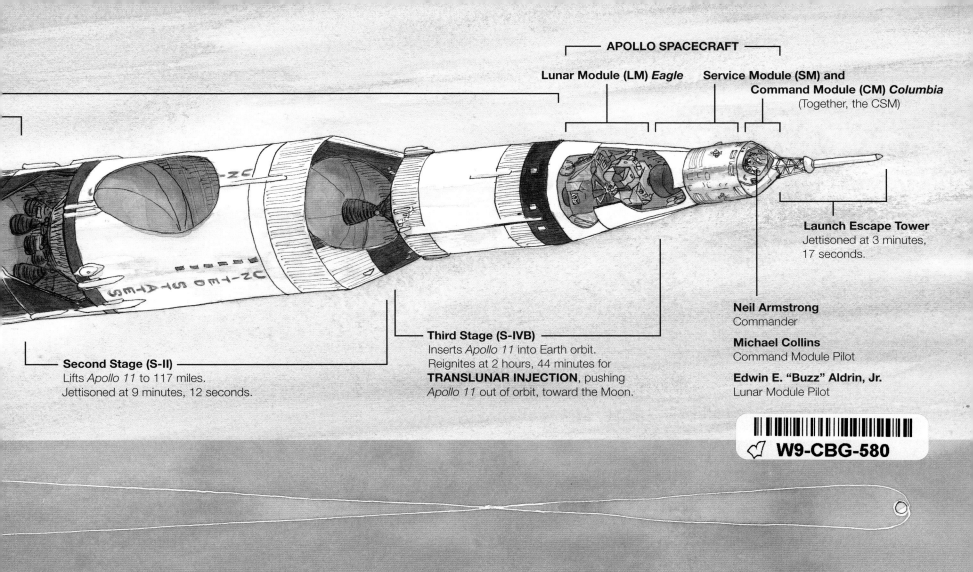

APOLLO SPACECRAFT

Lunar Module (LM) *Eagle*

Service Module (SM) and Command Module (CM) *Columbia*
(Together, the CSM)

Launch Escape Tower
Jettisoned at 3 minutes, 17 seconds.

Neil Armstrong
Commander

Michael Collins
Command Module Pilot

Edwin E. "Buzz" Aldrin, Jr.
Lunar Module Pilot

Second Stage (S-II)
Lifts *Apollo 11* to 117 miles.
Jettisoned at 9 minutes, 12 seconds.

Third Stage (S-IVB)
Inserts *Apollo 11* into Earth orbit.
Reignites at 2 hours, 44 minutes for
TRANSLUNAR INJECTION, pushing
Apollo 11 out of orbit, toward the Moon.

LUNAR LIFTOFF
Armstrong and Aldrin ride
the ascent stage of *Eagle*
up from Tranquility Base at
1:54 PM EDT on July 21.

Back in lunar orbit, the LM and CSM
dock. Armstrong and Aldrin rejoin
Collins in *Columbia*, bringing with them
lunar samples.

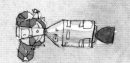

Eagle's ascent stage is then released . . .

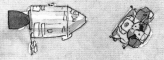

. . . and the CSM engine ignites for
TRANSEARTH INJECTION.

After a two-and-a-half-day
TRANSEARTH COAST *Apollo 11*
reaches Earth and jettisons the Service
Module.

ENTRY and LANDING
Columbia enters Earth's atmosphere . . .

. . . and splashes down safely at 12:50 PM
EDT on July 24.

The astronauts are taken by helicopter to the
USS *Hornet*, where they enter the Mobile
Quarantine Facility.

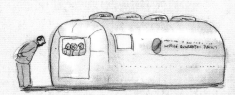

After three weeks in quarantine—and
with no sign of Moon germs—Armstrong,
Collins, and Aldrin are released to parades,
celebrations, and a goodwill tour of the
world.

For my parents

SOURCES

Andrew Chaikin's *A Man on the Moon* was, long ago now, my starting point for approaching the subject of the Apollo Moon missions. It is an accessible history of the program, from the fire that claimed the crew of *Apollo 1* to the accomplished lunar geology carried out by the crew of *Apollo 17*, with an emphasis on the experiences of the astronauts. *Carrying the Fire: An Astronaut's Journey* and *Liftoff: The Story of America's Adventure in Space*, both by Michael Collins, probably the best writer ever to ride a Saturn V, relate the experience of *Apollo 11*, specifically, and also outline the broader development of the space program. Norman Mailer's *Of a Fire on the Moon* gives a sense of *Apollo 11* in the context of the 1960s (for much of the book Mailer refers to himself in the third person as Aquarius) and also adroitly explains the mechanics of the flight (Mailer began his undergraduate work at Harvard as a student of aeronautical engineering). *Apollo: The Race to the Moon*, by Charles Murray and Catherine Bly Cox, tells the stories of the engineers who imagined and designed Apollo, and of the flight controllers who ran the missions. Also valuable were *First Man: The Life of Neil A. Armstrong*, by James R. Hansen, and *First on the Moon: A Voyage with Neil Armstrong, Michael Collins, and Edwin E. Aldrin, Jr.*, by Armstrong, Collins, and Aldrin, with Gene Farmer and Dora Jane Hamblin. For readers curious as to how all the pieces fit together in the strange craft of Apollo, *Virtual Apollo* and *Virtual LM*, by Scott P. Sullivan, offer a range of interior and exterior views.

The tremendous amount of diagrams, press releases, photographs, videos, flight plans, and memoranda that NASA makes available to the public were invaluable in the preparation of this book. Good starting points for viewing them are at http://spaceflight.nasa.gov/history/apollo/index.html and http://www.hq.nasa.gov/alsj/.

Useful films about Apollo included the documentaries *In the Shadow of the Moon* and, especially, Al Reinert's *For All Mankind*. The ten-plus hours of footage compiled in *Apollo 11: Men on the Moon*, from Spacecraft Films, might be only for people writing their own books about *Apollo 11*—but if you've got a yen for obscure snippets and real-time footage, this DVD is for you. Dramatizations of the missions, such as *Apollo 13* and the HBO series *From the Earth to the Moon*, had their place, as well. Archival CBS coverage of the landing, which I watched at the Paley Center for Media in New York, gave a sense of the excitement and suspense that attended the first landing. The footage is worth watching just to see Walter Cronkite at a loss for words immediately following the landing; to astronaut Wally Schirra, in the studio to help explain events to the viewers, an almost giddy Cronkite finally says, "Wally, say something."

Finally, visits to the Smithsonian National Air and Space Museum in Washington, DC, and the Johnson Space Center in Houston, Texas, allowed a firsthand look at mission tools, suits, machinery, and what is now known as "historic mission control." The visits also allowed a look at the actual vehicles of Apollo, overwhelming in their intricacy, boldness, and monumentality, and a fitting metaphor for the program as a whole.

Atheneum Books for Young Readers. An imprint of Simon & Schuster Children's Publishing Division. 1230 Avenue of the Americas, New York, New York 10020. Copyright © 2009 by Brian Floca. All rights reserved, including the right of reproduction in whole or in part in any form. Book design by Brian Floca and Michael McCartney. The text for this book is set in Helvetica Neue. The illustrations for this book are rendered in watercolor, ink, acrylic, and gouache. Manufactured in China.
10 9 8 7 6 5.   Library of Congress Cataloging-in-Publication Data. Floca, Brian. Moonshot : the flight of *Apollo 11* / written and illustrated by Brian Floca. p. cm. "A Richard Jackson book." ISBN-13: 978-1-4169-5046-2 ISBN-10: 1-4169-5046-X 1. Project Apollo (U.S.)—Juvenile literature. 2. *Apollo 11* (Spacecraft)—Juvenile literature. 3. Space flight to the moon—Juvenile literature. I. Title. TL789.8.U6F56 2008 629.45'4—dc22 2007052358

MOONSHOT

THE FLIGHT OF APOLLO 11 · BRIAN FLOCA

A Richard Jackson Book
Atheneum Books for Young Readers
New York London Toronto Sydney

High above
there is the Moon,
cold and quiet,
no air, no life,
but glowing in the sky.

Here below
there are three men

who close themselves
in special clothes,

who—*click*—lock hands
in heavy gloves,

who—*click*—lock heads
in large, round helmets.

It is summer here in Florida,
hot, and near the sea.
But now these men are dressed for colder, stranger places.
They walk with stiff and awkward steps
in suits not made for Earth.

They have studied and practiced and trained,
and said good-bye to family and friends.
If all goes well, they will be gone for one week,
gone where no one has been.

Their two small spaceships are
Columbia and *Eagle*.
They sit atop the rocket
that will raise them into space,
a monster of a machine:
It stands thirty stories,
it weighs six million pounds,
a tower full of fuel and fire
and valves and pipes and engines,
too big to believe, but built to fly—
the mighty, massive Saturn V.

The astronauts squeeze in
to *Columbia*'s sideways seats,
lying on their backs,
facing toward the sky—
Neil Armstrong on the left,
Michael Collins on the right,
Buzz Aldrin in the middle.

Click and they fasten straps.
Click and the hatch is sealed.

There they wait,
while the Saturn
hums beneath them.

Near the rocket, in Launch Control,
and far away in Houston, in Mission Control,
there are numbers, screens, and charts,
ways of watching and checking
every piece of the rocket and ships,
the fuel, the valves, the pipes, the engines,
the beats of the astronauts' hearts.

As the countdown closes,
each man watching is asked the question:
"GO/NO GO?"
And each man watching answers back:
"GO."
"GO."
"GO."
Apollo 11 is GO for launch.

10 . . . 9 . . . 8 . . . 7 . . .

Ignition sequence started. Flames
push hard against the pad,
every second pushing harder.

6 . . . 5 . . . 4 . . .

But still the rocket
does not rise.

Mighty arms
hold it steady . . .

hold it till the
countdown's finish . . .

3...2...1...

ZERO

LIFTOFF!

The rocket is released!
It rises
foot by foot,
it rises
pound by pound.

It climbs
the summer sky.
It rides a flapping,
cracking flame
and shakes the air,
and shakes the earth,
and makes a mighty

ROAR.

Armstrong, Collins, Aldrin
ride the fire and thunder
pressed deep in their seats,
their bodies as heavy as clay.

The rocket below them
sheds parts as it soars.
Bolts explode, engines ignite—
first stage, second stage, escape tower—
gone!

The rocket flies lighter,
the rocket flies faster;
in twelve minutes' time,
it's one hundred miles high.

Then, after an orbit around the Earth
to talk with Mission Control
to check the course
to check the rocket and ships,
the rocket's last stage fires again,
pushing the astronauts on.

And when the Earth
has rolled beneath
and rolled behind
and let the astronauts go,
the Saturn's last stage opens wide
and releases *Columbia*,
which was the rocket's tip,

and also *Eagle*, hidden till now,
a stranger ship, more bug than bird,
a black and gold and folded spider.

Michael Collins, *Columbia*'s pilot,
turns her back around . . .

. . . and locks *Columbia* to *Eagle*.

Then Armstrong, Collins, Aldrin
leave the last of the Saturn
and travel on in their
two small ships,
joined together,
flown as one.

They go rushing into darkness,
flying toward the Moon,
far away,
cold and quiet,
no air, no life,
but glowing in the sky.

Onboard *Columbia* and *Eagle*,
Armstrong, Collins, Aldrin
un*click* gloves,
un*click* helmets,
un*click* the straps
that hold them down,
and float inside their small ships,
their home for a week.

Here there is no up or down;
an astronaut can spin in air and
turn a floor into a wall
or a ceiling to a floor.

Here, on those sometimes
ceilings, walls, and floors—everywhere—
there are straps and screens and gauges,
buttons, handles, hoses,
and switches, switches, switches.

There are food and clothes
packed into corners.
There are flight plans, flashlights,
pens, and cameras—and they float too.
They drift from hands and pockets.
That's why there's Velcro everywhere:
for holding things so they stay put.

Here, where everything floats,
it takes some skill to eat a meal.
That ham salad sandwich? Watch the crumbs!
Soup? It comes in a bag, dry as dust.
Fix the bag to the water gun, fill it, mix it, stir it up.
Cream of chicken—not too bad!
(Better than the peanut cubes.)

Here, where everything floats,
it takes some skill to go to sleep.
There are no beds or pillows,
no night or day.
There is always, though,
the *hum* of circuits,
the *whir* of machines,
the thought of where you are,
and the thought of
where you're going.

And one more thing.
Here, where everything floats—everything—
it takes some skill to use the toilet.
(It takes pipes and hoses and bags.)
And there's no fresh air outside the window;
after a week this small home will not smell so good.

This is not why anyone
wants to be an astronaut.

But still ahead
there is the Moon,
    cold and quiet,
    no air, no life,
    but glowing in the sky.
    Glowing and growing,
    it takes them in,
    it pulls them close.

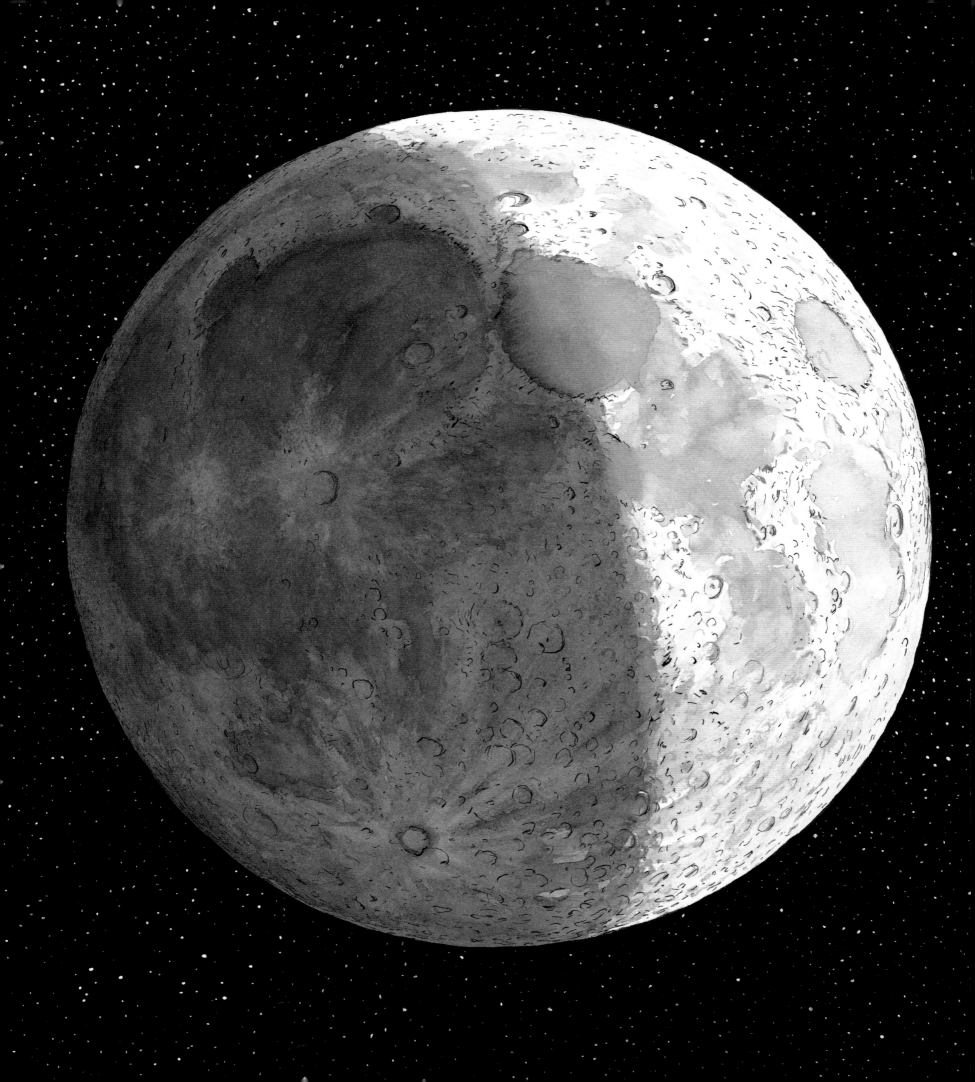

At the Moon,
Collins stays in *Columbia*,
high above,
a single circling soul.
Armstrong and Aldrin
leave in *Eagle*,
and take it low and lower.
They have just enough time
and just enough fuel.
They have a plan
and a place to land,
a chosen safe site
among the craters.

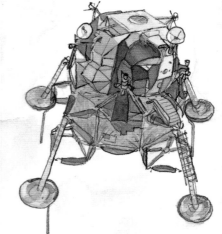

Now friends and strangers
in the distance, down below,
stay up late, get up early,
and stop as one
to watch and wait.
There are only maps and models to see;
there is no camera that can show the landing far away.

But what strange sounds there are to *hear*!
Whistles, beeps, and static,
strange new words and
quick, clipped news
of altitudes and speeds,
leaping across the dark
between Mission Control and the men
who are taking the *Eagle* to land on the Moon,
who are going where no one has been.

Onboard *Eagle*,
Aldrin calls out information
while Armstrong steers the ship.
They fly low and lower, looking,
looking for their landing site.

But now *Eagle*, they see, has flown too far.
They are miles from where they mean to be,
and below their small and spindly ship
they see no level place,
only broken stone and rock,
only shadows in deep craters
on the great and growing Moon.

Far from home and far from help,
still steady, steady,
the astronauts fly
till time and fuel are running out.

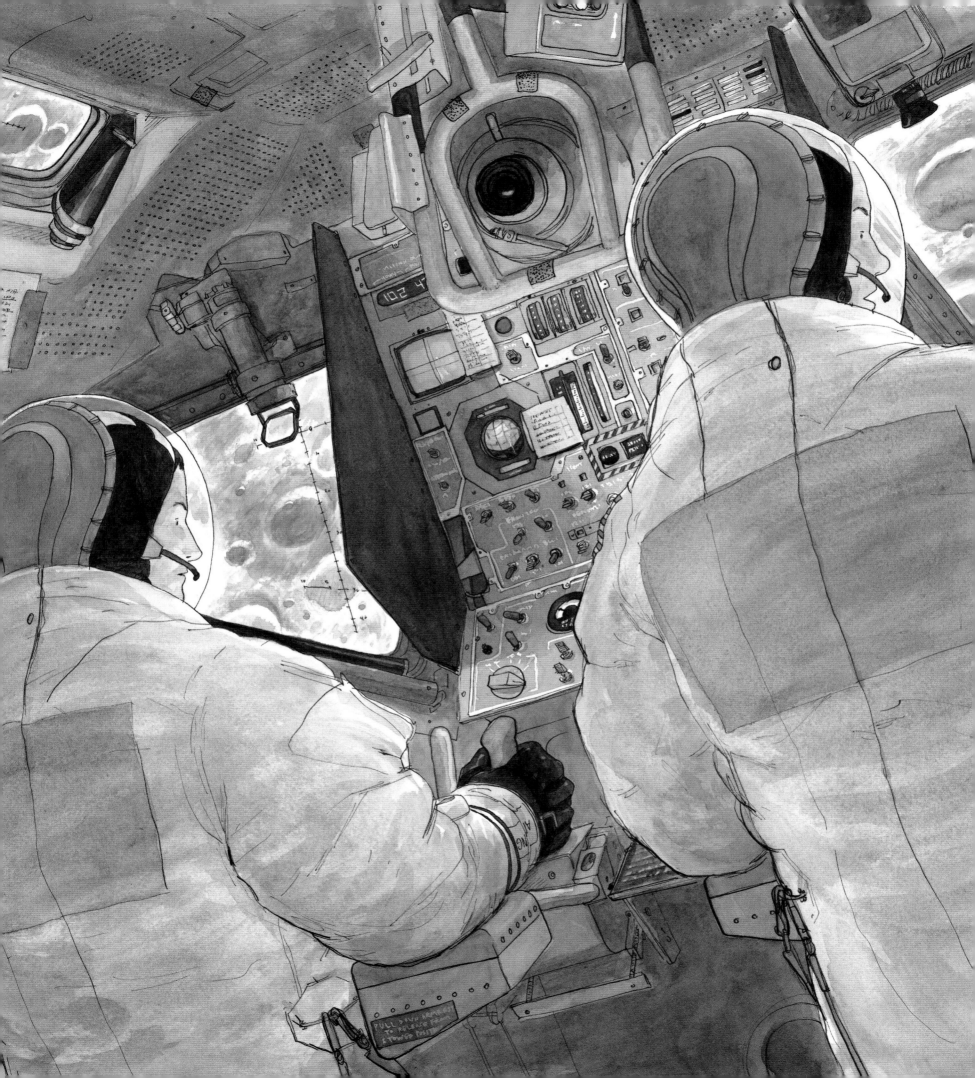

Then . . . there! Clean and flat, not too far!
Sixty seconds left! Armstrong fires the rockets.
Eagle slows and lower goes until a spray of dust,
a bloom of moon, flowers up around her.
Slow and slower,
low and lower,
low and lower—
landing!

And far away,
where friends and strangers lean to listen,
where friends and strangers lean to hear,
there comes a distant voice:
Armstrong, calling from the Moon,
calm as a man who just parked a car.
"Houston," he says. "Tranquility Base here. The *Eagle* has landed."

Armstrong is calm—but on Earth they cheer!

Then Armstrong and Aldrin
climb down from the *Eagle*
in heavy gloves, in large, round helmets,
in suits not made for Earth—

—in suits made for the Moon,
here below, all around them,
cold and quiet,
no air, but life—
there is life
on the strange and silent,
magnificent Moon.

Armstrong and Aldrin
walk its rough, wide places.
They step, they hop.
As light as boys,
they lope, they leap!

In the dust and stone
beneath their feet,
no seed has ever grown,
no root has ever reached.
Still secrets wait there,
the story of the Moon:

Where did it come from?
How old is it?
What is it made of?
(Not green cheese.)

And up above
the ash-gray plains,
the sky is pitch and empty,
and all the stars stay hidden:
That is how bright the Moon is
when you are standing on its face.

But in that blank and starless sky . . .

. . . high above
there is the Earth,
rushing oceans, racing clouds,
swaying fields and forests.
Family, friends, and strangers,
everyone you've ever known,
everyone you might—
the good and lonely Earth,
glowing in the sky.

When their work is done,
Armstrong, Collins, Aldrin
fly back together from the Moon,

which rolls beneath,
which rolls behind,
letting them loose,
letting them go.

They fly back together through the dark
with pictures, stones, and stories,
with secrets of the sky,
with a view of home,
from far away.

Back to family,
back to friends,
to warmth,
to light,
to trees
and blue water.
Back from the Moon,
  they land with a

SPLASH!

To warmth,
to light,
to home at last.

ONE GIANT LEAP

"First, I believe that this nation should commit itself to achieving the goal, before this decade is out, of landing a man on the Moon and returning him safely to the Earth."

So President John F. Kennedy stated his goals for the United States in space in May of 1961. The Moon was a formidable target for a nation that could not yet lift a man into orbit around the Earth, but Kennedy had reason to be ambitious. In the new race to explore space, the United States found itself, again and again, squarely behind the achievements of the Soviet Union, and Kennedy had begun to look for an achievement in space that could be important to exploration, that would be dramatic enough to make an impression in the eyes of the world, and that the United States had a fighting chance of accomplishing first.

Kennedy's advisors let him know that the Soviets would hold clear advantages in certain efforts, such as putting manned laboratories into orbit. But there were other goals, they told him, further out, that the United States might yet be first to realize—including a trip to the Moon. Certainly, there was a power and even a certain graspable simplicity to the idea of a Moon voyage, an idea which had exerted a pull on storytellers, fabulists, and explorers for as long as tales had been told. But could it be done? Could it be done within nine years? How?

Serious advocates of space exploration and science fiction films alike (and Hergé's Tintin adventure *Destination Moon*, too) had made familiar the picture of a rocket resting on tail fins on the lunar surface, ready to return, whole, to Earth. It was a compelling image, but lifting into space a giant ship that could travel intact to and from the Moon would have required truly gigantic new rockets, rockets which likely could not have been developed within Kennedy's deadline.

Engineers instead began to imagine reaching the Moon with small, specialized craft. Relatively light to begin with, these ships would be able to reduce their weight further by shedding parts of themselves during the missions. They would require maneuvers that some considered dangerous, such as rendezvousing over the Moon, but the advantages that their weight offered carried the argument, and soon the vehicles of Apollo were taking shape. The spacecraft would consist of a Command Module and a Service Module (together, the CSM) and, for actually getting astronauts to and from the Moon's surface, a Lunar Excursion Module. (The name was later simplified to Lunar Module, or LM, out of concern that "Excursion" sounded too casual.) The launch vehicle needed to raise even these small ships to the Moon, the Saturn V rocket, would still have to be enormous, but it, too, would shed its own weight as it went; it would in fact dismantle itself as it flew. The result was the incredible shrinking *Apollo 11*, an assembly of machinery that left Earth the size of a skyscraper—363 feet in height, and almost six and a half million pounds in weight—and that returned the size of a Volkswagen bus.

Apollo 11's tricks of reduction began just two minutes after launch on the morning of July 16, 1969. By that time the Saturn V had already lifted astronauts Neil Armstrong, Michael Collins, and Edwin "Buzz" Aldrin, Jr., forty miles into the sky and, in doing so, had emptied the fuel from its gigantic first-stage booster tank. Explosive bolts then released the first stage, sending it tumbling in a long arc into the Atlantic Ocean, halfway between Florida and Bermuda. The second stage then ignited and burned for six minutes, long enough to push *Apollo 11* to roughly one hundred twenty miles above the Earth. Then that stage, too, was jettisoned, left to fall southwest of the Azores. The third stage put the rocket into orbit around the Earth. A little over two hours later, after a review by the crew and Mission Control, the third stage fired again and sent *Apollo 11* toward the Moon.

Shortly afterwards, the joined Command and Service Modules separated from the third stage. As the CSM pulled forward, the panels that made up the cone of the Saturn's third stage parted like so many petals, revealing the Lunar Module *Eagle*. Michael Collins, the CSM pilot, docked the CSM with the LM, and the two ships left the last of the once enormous Saturn V.

As they left Earth orbit the astronauts traveled at a speed of 25,000 miles an hour—almost seven miles a second—but they were slowing as they flew. Like a ball thrown high into the air, *Apollo 11* was leaving Earth but still felt its tug. By the time the astronauts were within 40,000 miles of the Moon, their speed had been reduced to 2,000 miles per hour. But before they could begin the long fall back, they entered the gravitational influence of the Moon; it pulled them forward, and *Apollo 11* gained speed once again.

On July 19 the crew fired the CSM's large bell engine in the direction of their flight, slowing themselves enough to enter lunar orbit. The next day Armstrong and Aldrin undocked *Eagle* from *Columbia* and began their descent to their landing site.

Up to this point, the crew of *Apollo 11* had traveled paths tested by previous crews. In the one-step-leads-to-the-next manner of the program, *Apollo 8* had first left Earth to orbit the Moon; *Apollo 9* had first tested and rendezvoused Command and Lunar Modules; and the crew of *Apollo 10* had taken their Command and Lunar Modules (dubbed *Charlie Brown* and *Snoopy*, respectively) to the Moon and flown within nine miles of the surface. Now the final task fell to Armstrong, Aldrin, and the team at Mission Control: to set a strange new ship on a strange new world—to land on the Moon.

The flight down was not smooth. There were communication glitches, obscurely coded computer alarms, errors in *Eagle*'s course (the ship ended up four miles downrange from its intended landing site), and, finally, the threat of low fuel and of a late, dangerous abort to the flight. The astronauts and Mission Control handled it all with trademark cool, but there was